The Money Magnet Blueprint

The Money Magnet Blueprint

Matthew Petchinsky

1

The Money Magnet Blueprint: Unlocking Unlimited Wealth By: Matthew Petchinsky

Introduction: The Psychology and Strategies Behind Attracting Financial Abundance

Money is more than just currency—it is energy, opportunity, and the reflection of our mindset. Financial abundance is not merely a matter of luck or external circumstances but a direct result of our beliefs, habits, and actions. If you've ever wondered why some people seem to effortlessly attract wealth while others struggle despite their best efforts, the answer lies in psychology and strategy.

The *Money Magnet Blueprint* is not just about making money—it's about reshaping your entire relationship with wealth so that money flows to you naturally and consistently. This introduction will delve into the psychology behind financial abundance and the strategic steps necessary to unlock unlimited wealth.

The Psychology of Financial Abundance

The foundation of financial success begins in the mind. Before money manifests in your life, you must first align your beliefs, emotions, and subconscious patterns with prosperity. Let's explore the key psychological principles that influence wealth attraction.

1. The Subconscious Mind and Wealth Programming

Your subconscious mind controls up to 95% of your daily decisions, habits, and behaviors. The way you think about money—whether you see it as an abundant resource or a scarce commodity—determines how much of it you attract or repel.

From childhood, many people are conditioned with limiting beliefs such as:

- "Money is the root of all evil."
- "Rich people are greedy or dishonest."
- "It's hard to make money."
- "I don't deserve wealth."

These subconscious scripts shape your financial reality. If deep down you associate money with struggle or guilt, you will subconsciously sabotage opportunities for wealth. Reprogramming these beliefs through affirmations, visualization, and neuro-linguistic programming (NLP) is essential to becoming a true money magnet.

2. The Law of Attraction and Money Manifestation

The Law of Attraction states that like attracts like. If you constantly dwell on financial lack, stress about bills, and worry about scarcity, you send signals to the universe (and your subconscious) that reinforce financial struggle.

To shift into abundance, you must:

- **Focus on gratitude:** Appreciate the money you already have, no matter how small. Gratitude amplifies abundance.
- **Visualize your financial goals:** Picture your bank account growing, your dream home, and the life of financial freedom you desire.
- **Use powerful affirmations:** Statements like “Money flows to me easily and effortlessly” help rewire your subconscious.

3. Emotional Frequency and Wealth Alignment

Your emotional state influences your ability to attract money. If you are constantly stressed, anxious, or fearful about finances, you are operating from a low vibration that repels wealth. On the other hand, feelings of joy, confidence, and abundance create a magnetic field that draws financial opportunities.

Train yourself to cultivate emotions that align with financial success. This can be done through:

- Meditation
- Mindfulness practices
- Surrounding yourself with wealthy, positive-minded individuals
- Engaging in activities that make you feel abundant

Strategies for Attracting Financial Abundance

While mindset is crucial, action is what turns financial dreams into reality. Here are proven strategies that will transform your financial life:

1. The Power of Financial Clarity

Before wealth can flow into your life, you must have a clear vision of what you want. Set precise financial goals, such as:

- Earning $100,000 per year
- Generating passive income streams
- Becoming debt-free
- Investing in real estate or stocks

When your goals are specific and measurable, your brain actively seeks ways to achieve them.

2. High-Income Skills and Wealth Multiplication

Relying on a single source of income limits your financial potential. The wealthiest individuals develop **high-income skills** that allow them to multiply their earnings, such as:

- Sales and persuasion
- Copywriting
- Investing
- Entrepreneurship
- Digital marketing

Mastering these skills ensures you are always in control of your financial destiny.

3. Multiple Streams of Income

The average millionaire has **at least seven streams of income**. Instead of depending on one job, diversify your earnings through:

- Passive income (real estate, dividend stocks, digital products)
- Side businesses
- High-yield investments
- Royalties and licensing deals

By creating multiple streams of income, you secure financial stability and freedom.

4. Smart Money Management and Financial Discipline

Wealth is not just about making money—it's about keeping it and growing it. Follow the **80/20 Rule**:

- Invest at least **20%** of your income into assets that generate passive income.
- Live off **80% or less** while building your financial empire.

Budgeting, cutting unnecessary expenses, and avoiding debt traps will fast-track your journey to abundance.

5. The Power of Generosity and Wealth Circulation

Many people hoard money out of fear, which ironically blocks financial flow. Wealthy individuals understand that **money is energy**, and circulation brings more of it.

By giving to charity, tipping generously, and supporting others, you open channels for even greater financial blessings to come your way. The key is to give with joy, knowing that money flows back multiplied.

Final Thoughts: Becoming a True Money Magnet

The *Money Magnet Blueprint* is not just about attracting wealth but transforming yourself into the kind of person who naturally generates financial abundance. By combining the right mindset with strategic action, you will unlock unlimited wealth and create a life of financial freedom.

As you embark on this journey, remember: **your thoughts shape your reality, your emotions fuel your manifestations, and your actions determine your financial destiny.** Wealth is already within your reach—you simply need to align with it and claim what is yours.

Now, let's dive into the blueprint and start attracting the financial abundance you deserve!

Chapter 1: Breaking Free from Scarcity Mindset

Our financial reality is a direct reflection of our mindset. If you have ever felt stuck in a cycle of living paycheck to paycheck, struggling to save, or constantly feeling like there is "never enough," then you may be trapped in a **scarcity mindset**. This limiting belief system keeps many people from achieving financial success because it conditions the mind to expect lack instead of abundance.

In this chapter, we will explore how the scarcity mindset develops, the psychological effects it has on financial decisions, and practical steps to break free from it. By shifting to an abundance mentality, you can begin attracting wealth effortlessly and create lasting financial freedom.

The Roots of Scarcity Thinking

Scarcity thinking is not something we are born with—it is learned. Many of our financial behaviors and beliefs stem from childhood conditioning, societal programming, and past financial experiences. Understanding where these beliefs come from is the first step in breaking free from them.

1. Childhood Conditioning and Money Beliefs

Think about the messages you heard about money growing up. Did your parents or guardians frequently say things like:

- "Money doesn't grow on trees."
- "We can't afford that."
- "Rich people are greedy."
- "You have to work hard just to get by."

These statements create deep-seated mental associations between money and struggle. If your upbringing was filled with financial stress, you may have unconsciously adopted the belief that money is difficult to obtain or that wanting more is selfish.

2. Society's Influence on Scarcity Thinking

Modern society reinforces scarcity thinking through media, advertising, and cultural narratives. We are constantly bombarded with messages of financial crisis, economic instability, and the illusion that wealth is only for the lucky or elite.

- The **news cycle** often highlights financial downturns, layoffs, and recessions, creating fear around money.
- **Advertising** preys on scarcity by making people feel like they are missing out unless they buy something.
- The **education system** rarely teaches financial literacy, leaving most people unprepared to build wealth.

When we internalize these messages, we begin to operate from a mindset of fear rather than opportunity, reinforcing financial limitations.

3. Personal Financial Struggles and Trauma

Past financial failures or struggles can also reinforce a scarcity mindset. If you have experienced job loss, debt, or unexpected financial hardships, you may subconsciously associate money with stress, failure, or insecurity.

- You might develop **risk aversion**, avoiding investments or opportunities because of past losses.
- You could suffer from **"learned helplessness,"** believing that no matter what you do, your financial situation will not improve.
- You may engage in **self-sabotage**, rejecting wealth opportunities due to an underlying belief that you are not "meant" to be wealthy.

Recognizing these patterns is essential to rewriting your financial story.

How the Scarcity Mindset Affects Your Financial Reality

A scarcity mindset doesn't just keep you poor—it actively pushes wealth away. Here's how it manifests in your financial behaviors:

1. Fear-Based Decision Making

Scarcity-minded individuals make financial choices out of fear instead of logic or strategy. This can include:

- Keeping all money in a savings account instead of investing, out of fear of loss.
- Settling for a low-paying job because the idea of switching careers feels too risky.
- Hoarding money and never spending, believing there will never be "enough."

2. Living Paycheck to Paycheck

Even if someone earns a decent salary, a scarcity mindset often leads to poor money management. They may:

- Spend everything they make instead of saving or investing.
- Avoid budgeting because they don't want to confront their financial reality.
- Constantly feel like money is slipping through their fingers.

3. Rejecting Wealth Opportunities

One of the most damaging effects of scarcity thinking is missing out on opportunities to increase wealth. When you believe money is hard to come by, you may:

- Avoid starting a business or side hustle because of the "risk."
- Refuse to negotiate a higher salary or raise.
- Turn down investment opportunities due to fear of losing money.

Breaking Free from the Scarcity Mindset

Shifting from scarcity to abundance requires intentional effort and daily practice. Below are powerful strategies to help you break free from limiting beliefs and rewire your brain for financial success.

1. Rewire Your Money Beliefs

Since the scarcity mindset is deeply ingrained, the first step is to **re-program your subconscious mind** with new beliefs about money.

A. Challenge and Replace Limiting Beliefs

Write down every negative belief you have about money, and then counteract each one with a positive affirmation.

Scarcity Thought	Abundance Replacement
"Money is hard to make."	"Money flows to me effortlessly."
"I'm not good with money."	"I am mastering financial abundance."
"I'll never be rich."	"I am becoming wealthier every day."

Repeat these affirmations daily to shift your inner narrative.

B. Visualize Financial Abundance

Your mind cannot differentiate between imagined and real experiences. Spend a few minutes each day visualizing yourself:

- Receiving large checks or bank deposits.
- Living in your dream home, debt-free.
- Generating passive income effortlessly.

The more real it feels, the faster you will attract it into your reality.

2. Practice Gratitude for Money

Gratitude is the fastest way to shift your energy from lack to abundance. Instead of focusing on what you don't have, appreciate the money you **do** have.

- Start a **gratitude journal** and write down five things about money you are grateful for daily.
- Every time you pay a bill, say: "I am grateful for the ability to afford this."
- Acknowledge even small amounts of income as evidence that money is flowing to you.

This rewires your brain to see abundance everywhere, making you a magnet for wealth.

3. Create an Abundance-Oriented Financial Plan

To fully step into abundance, your financial actions must align with your new mindset.

A. Set Clear Financial Goals

Instead of saying, "I want to be rich," set specific, measurable goals:
◈ "I will earn $10,000 per month through multiple income streams."
◈ "I will save $50,000 in the next 12 months."
◈ "I will invest 20% of my income into wealth-building assets."

Having clear targets activates your brain's **Reticular Activating System (RAS)**, which filters opportunities that align with your goals.

B. Build Multiple Streams of Income

Wealthy individuals don't rely on a single paycheck. Start by adding:

- A **side hustle** or freelance work.
- Passive income sources like **digital products, investments, or real estate**.
- Monetizing skills through **consulting, online courses, or social media content creation**.

The more income streams you create, the more financially secure you become.

C. Shift from Consumer to Creator Mindset

Instead of thinking, **"How can I save more?"**, start asking, **"How can I create more wealth?"**

- Focus on **value creation** instead of just cutting costs.
- Invest in **self-education and skill-building** for higher earning potential.
- Learn how **money works** so you can **multiply** it instead of fearing it.

Final Thoughts: Reclaiming Your Financial Power

Breaking free from a scarcity mindset is **not an overnight process**, but every small shift in thinking creates momentum. By changing your internal dialogue, practicing gratitude, and aligning your actions with wealth-building strategies, you will rewire your financial reality.

This chapter is the first step toward transforming your financial life.

Your journey to financial abundance starts **now**. The choice is yours—will you remain in scarcity, or will you claim your birthright to **unlimited wealth**?

Chapter 2: The Science of Wealth Attraction

Wealth is not just a result of hard work—it is a combination of **mindset, strategy, and opportunity.** The most financially successful individuals don't just make money; they **attract** it. They have developed a wealth-attraction mindset that enables them to recognize and capitalize on opportunities with confidence.

In this chapter, we will explore the science behind wealth attraction, the psychological and neurological factors that influence financial success, and actionable strategies to develop an abundance-focused mindset. You will learn how to rewire your brain for prosperity, shift from passive wishful thinking to intentional wealth-building, and take advantage of financial opportunities without fear or hesitation.

The Science Behind Wealth Attraction

At its core, wealth attraction is based on **psychological principles, neuroscience, and behavioral economics.** Understanding these concepts will allow you to harness them to your advantage.

1. The Reticular Activating System (RAS) and Financial Awareness

The **Reticular Activating System (RAS)** is a part of your brain that acts as a filter for information. It determines what you focus on based on your beliefs, experiences, and subconscious programming.

Have you ever decided to buy a new car and suddenly started seeing that model everywhere? That's your **RAS at work.** The same principle applies to money:

- If you **believe wealth is hard to attain,** your RAS will filter out wealth opportunities.
- If you **train your brain to recognize financial abundance,** you will start seeing new ways to make and attract money.

How to Activate Your RAS for Wealth

To program your RAS to focus on financial abundance, try these exercises:

◈ **Wealth Affirmations:** Repeat daily statements like *"I see financial opportunities everywhere."*

◈ **Visualization:** Spend 5 minutes each morning picturing yourself achieving your financial goals.

◈ **Journaling:** Write down three money-making ideas daily to train your brain to seek solutions.

By consistently feeding your mind with **wealth-focused thoughts,** your RAS will begin filtering in opportunities that align with your goals.

2. The Law of Cause and Effect: Wealth is Predictable

Many believe wealth is random or luck-based, but it follows the universal law of **cause and effect**—every financial outcome is the result of specific actions.

- Wealthy individuals make **calculated decisions** that yield high returns.
- Financially struggling people often engage in habits that keep them in a cycle of lack.

To **reverse-engineer** success, study the habits of wealthy individuals and adopt their behaviors.

Common Habits of Wealthy People:

⟐ They **invest** instead of just saving.
⟐ They **focus on value creation** rather than just earning a paycheck.
⟐ They **embrace risk with strategy** instead of fearing it.
⟐ They **surround themselves with successful people** who elevate their mindset.

By aligning your actions with proven wealth-building strategies, financial success becomes a **predictable outcome rather than a random event.**

3. The Role of Emotional Frequency in Wealth Attraction

Your emotions **emit energy frequencies** that attract similar experiences. When you feel abundant, you attract more abundance. When you operate from fear, scarcity, or stress, you repel wealth.

How Emotions Influence Your Financial Reality:

- **Fear and scarcity** = Hesitating on wealth opportunities, playing small.
- **Confidence and abundance** = Taking bold action, seizing opportunities.
- **Gratitude and joy** = Attracting more financial blessings.

◈ **Practical Exercise:** Whenever you feel anxious about money, shift your emotional state by:

- Practicing **deep breathing** or meditation.
- Listening to music that uplifts you.
- Writing a gratitude list about money (even small amounts count).

By **maintaining a high emotional frequency,** you naturally attract wealth-building opportunities.

Developing a Wealth Attraction Mindset

Shifting from a **scarcity mindset** to a **wealth attraction mindset** requires rewiring your thought patterns, beliefs, and behaviors. Here's how to make the transformation:

1. Shift from "How Can I Save?" to "How Can I Create?"

Most people focus on **cutting costs** to feel financially secure, but the truly wealthy prioritize **creating new income streams.**

◈ **Scarcity Thinking:** "I need to stop spending money."
◈ **Wealth Thinking:** "How can I increase my income?"

◈ **Exercise:** Each day, write down 3 ways you could generate an extra $1,000 this month. This could include:

- Selling a product or service
- Monetizing a skill
- Investing in a new venture

This simple shift in focus **expands your financial possibilities** instead of limiting them.

2. Train Your Brain to See Opportunities Instead of Risks

Many people **avoid** financial opportunities because of fear. Wealthy individuals understand that **risk and opportunity are two sides of the same coin.**

How to Overcome Financial Fear:

◈ **Educate Yourself:** The more you understand money, the less intimidating it becomes. Read books on investing, entrepreneurship, and wealth-building.

◈ **Take Small Risks First:** Start with small investments to build confidence.

◈ **Adopt the "Fail Forward" Mentality:** Instead of fearing mistakes, **view them as learning experiences** that bring you closer to success.

◈ **Exercise:** Write down one financial opportunity you've hesitated to pursue. Challenge yourself to take action within the next 7 days.

3. Surround Yourself with Wealth-Oriented People

Your **environment shapes your mindset.** If you spend time around people who complain about money and believe success is impossible, their mindset will rub off on you.

◈ **Find a Wealth-Minded Community:** Join mastermind groups, networking events, or online communities where people discuss wealth-building.

◈ **Study Success Stories:** Read autobiographies of self-made millionaires to shift your perspective on what is possible.

◈ **Limit Exposure to Negativity:** Reduce time spent consuming fear-based media about financial struggles.

◈ **Challenge:** Identify **one financially successful person** you admire. Follow their work, study their habits, and adopt at least **one** of their strategies.

Taking Advantage of Financial Opportunities with Confidence

Developing a wealth attraction mindset is meaningless if you don't **act on financial opportunities.** Here's how to ensure you confidently seize the right opportunities:

1. Identify and Evaluate Opportunities Quickly

Wealthy individuals don't wait for "perfect" conditions—they take action **before** others see the opportunity.

How to Evaluate an Opportunity:

◈ **Does it align with your financial goals?** If it moves you toward wealth, consider it.

◈ **What is the risk-to-reward ratio?** If the upside is high, take calculated risks.

◈ **Is there a proven success model?** Learn from those who have done it before.

◈ **Action Step:** Research and list **three wealth-building opportunities** available to you right now (e.g., starting an online business, investing in stocks, selling a digital product). Choose one and commit to taking action.

2. Adopt the "Speed of Implementation" Rule

The wealthiest individuals **act fast** when they recognize financial potential. They don't waste time overanalyzing or doubting themselves.

◈ **Rule:** When you learn about a valuable financial opportunity, take at least **one action step within 24 hours.**

◈ **Example:** If you discover a profitable side hustle, set up a simple landing page or make your first sale **immediately.**

◈ **Exercise:** Make a commitment to act on the next financial opportunity you encounter within **24 hours.**

Final Thoughts: Becoming a Wealth Magnet

Attracting wealth is not about luck—it's about **mindset, awareness, and action.** By rewiring your brain for abundance, training yourself to see opportunities, and taking decisive action, you will naturally draw money and success into your life.

Your financial future starts now. Shift your mindset, seize opportunities with confidence, and **watch how effortlessly wealth begins flowing to you.**

Chapter 3: Developing High-Income Skills

In today's world, financial security is no longer guaranteed by simply having a job. If you want to achieve long-term wealth and financial independence, you must develop **high-income skills**—skills that allow you to generate significant income regardless of your circumstances, economic downturns, or job market fluctuations.

This chapter will explore the most **valuable high-income skills**, how to develop them, and how to monetize them effectively. Additionally, we will cover **practical money management strategies** that will ensure financial security and long-term wealth growth, helping you transition from earning money to **keeping and multiplying it.**

What Are High-Income Skills?

A **high-income skill** is a specialized ability that allows you to earn **at least $10,000 per month** or more. These skills typically:

◈ Have a **high market demand.**
◈ Are **scalable**, meaning you can earn more over time.
◈ Offer **financial independence** by allowing you to work on your own terms.

Unlike traditional jobs where you trade time for money, **high-income skills let you leverage expertise to generate unlimited income.**

Why High-Income Skills Are the Key to Wealth

Many people rely on **fixed-income jobs**, meaning they earn based on set salaries or hourly wages. This creates financial limitations because:

- **Your income is capped** by your employer.
- **You must work more hours to earn more money.**
- **Job security is uncertain** in changing economic conditions.

High-income skills, on the other hand, allow you to:
◈ **Earn more while working less** (higher pay per hour).
◈ **Create multiple income streams** (freelancing, consulting, selling digital products).
◈ **Become recession-proof**, as valuable skills are always in demand.

The secret to **attracting financial abundance** isn't working harder—it's **working smarter by mastering high-income skills.**

Top High-Income Skills to Master

Here are the **most valuable high-income skills** you can develop to build long-term financial security.

1. Sales and Persuasion

- **Why It's Valuable:** Sales drive every business in the world. Companies and entrepreneurs are always looking for people who can **sell products, close deals, and increase revenue.**
- **How to Learn It:**
  ◈ Study sales psychology (*books: "The Psychology of Selling" by Brian Tracy*).
  ◈ Take online courses on **copywriting, negotiation, and persuasion.**
  ◈ Practice selling a product or service and refine your pitch.
- **Ways to Monetize It:**
  ◈ Work as a **high-ticket closer** for businesses.
  ◈ Sell digital or physical products.
  ◈ Offer sales consulting or coaching.

2. Copywriting (Persuasive Writing for Sales & Marketing)

- **Why It's Valuable:** Copywriting is the skill of writing **persuasive words** that get people to buy products, sign up for services, or take action.
- **How to Learn It:**
  ◈ Study proven sales copy techniques (*book: "Breakthrough Advertising" by Eugene Schwartz*).
  ◈ Practice writing email sequences, landing pages, and product descriptions.
  ◈ Analyze successful marketing campaigns.
- **Ways to Monetize It:**
  ◈ Freelance for businesses needing sales copy.
  ◈ Write **advertisements, website content, and social media posts.**
  ◈ Create and sell **your own digital marketing courses.**

3. Digital Marketing & Social Media Growth

- **Why It's Valuable:** Businesses need **online visibility** to grow. Digital marketers help companies reach customers through social media, SEO, paid ads, and content marketing.
- **How to Learn It:**
  ⟐ Take online courses on **Facebook ads, Google ads, and SEO.**
  ⟐ Run marketing experiments on a personal blog or Instagram account.
  ⟐ Study analytics to measure campaign success.
- **Ways to Monetize It:**
  ⟐ Offer digital marketing services to businesses.
  ⟐ Sell online courses teaching marketing strategies.
  ⟐ Grow and monetize **social media pages** (YouTube, Instagram, TikTok).

4. Investing & Financial Literacy

- **Why It's Valuable:** Learning how money works ensures you **keep and multiply your wealth.**
- **How to Learn It:**
  ◈ Study books on **investing, real estate, and stocks** (*book: "The Intelligent Investor" by Benjamin Graham*).
  ◈ Follow financial mentors who **teach wealth-building strategies.**
  ◈ Start with small investments and scale over time.
- **Ways to Monetize It:**
  ◈ Invest in **stocks, cryptocurrency, and real estate.**
  ◈ Teach **financial literacy courses** or coach clients.
  ◈ Build a **personal finance YouTube channel or blog.**

5. Public Speaking & Personal Branding

- **Why It's Valuable:** Public speaking builds **authority and credibility**, allowing you to **attract opportunities** like consulting, coaching, and brand sponsorships.
- **How to Learn It:**
  ◈ Practice speaking on video (start a YouTube or TikTok channel).
  ◈ Join **public speaking groups** (like Toastmasters).
  ◈ Learn storytelling techniques to **connect with audiences.**
- **Ways to Monetize It:**
  ◈ Get paid for **speaking engagements.**
  ◈ Offer **personal branding coaching.**
  ◈ Build and sell **courses on confidence and public speaking.**

Practical Money Management Strategies for Financial Security

Developing a high-income skill is **only half the battle**—you must also **manage money wisely** to ensure long-term wealth growth.

1. Follow the 50/30/20 Rule

This simple budget system ensures financial stability:

- **50% for necessities** (housing, food, transportation).
- **30% for lifestyle spending** (entertainment, travel).
- **20% for investments and savings** (stocks, business, retirement).

If you have **high debt**, increase **your savings to 30%** and **reduce lifestyle spending.**

2. Pay Yourself First (Automatic Savings Strategy)

Instead of spending first and saving later, reverse the process:

◈ Set up an **automatic transfer** that moves **20% of your income into savings or investments.**

◈ Treat saving like a **non-negotiable bill**—pay yourself before anyone else.

3. Build Multiple Income Streams

High-income skills allow you to **earn more**, but true wealth comes from **diversifying income sources.**

3 Core Wealth Streams:

1◈ **Active Income** – What you earn from work (freelancing, sales, coaching).
2◈ **Passive Income** – Income from investments (stocks, real estate, online courses).
3◈ **Business Income** – Revenue from selling products/services.

The goal is to **shift from active to passive income** over time so money works for you.

4. Protect Your Money: Emergency Fund & Insurance

◈ **Emergency Fund:** Save at least **3-6 months of expenses** in a separate account.
◈ **Invest in Insurance:** Health, life, and income protection insurance provide financial security in unexpected situations.

Final Thoughts: Mastering Wealth Growth

Developing high-income skills **empowers you to earn at will**, but financial security comes from **managing and multiplying wealth wisely.**

◈ **Your next steps:**
◈ Choose **one high-income skill** from this list and commit to learning it.
◈ Set a **monthly financial goal** and track your progress.
◈ Start **applying money management strategies** to build long-term wealth.

By taking control of your **skills and financial habits,** you will create **unlimited income potential and financial security for life.**

Chapter 4: How Millionaires Manage Their Time and Money

Wealth isn't just about how much money you make—it's about how **effectively** you manage your time and money. The difference between struggling financially and becoming a millionaire often comes down to **how you prioritize your hours and where you allocate your money.**

Millionaires don't just work harder—they work **smarter.** They manage their time in a way that **multiplies productivity** and make financial decisions that **compound wealth over time.**

In this chapter, we'll break down:

◈ How millionaires **structure their days** for maximum efficiency.
◈ The **money management habits** that lead to financial success.
◈ Powerful **investment strategies** that will grow your wealth and create **generational financial freedom.**

By implementing these principles, you will not only increase your income but **secure long-term wealth** for yourself and future generations.

How Millionaires Manage Their Time

Time is the **most valuable resource**—far more than money. Millionaires know that **how they spend their time determines their financial future.**

1. The Millionaire Mindset: Time is an Asset, Not an Expense

Most people think of time in terms of **hours traded for money** (jobs, gigs, hourly pay). Millionaires see time as an **investment**—something that, when used wisely, **creates wealth automatically.**

The biggest mindset shift:

◈ **Poor mindset:** "How can I make money today?"

◈ **Wealthy mindset:** "How can I build assets that make money for me over time?"

This shift forces you to focus on **scalability, delegation, and high-impact activities** rather than being stuck in a cycle of trading time for cash.

2. The 80/20 Rule: Focus on What Actually Creates Wealth

Millionaires **prioritize tasks that have the highest impact.** This follows the **Pareto Principle (80/20 Rule)—80% of results come from 20% of activities.**

◈ **How to apply the 80/20 Rule:**

◈ Identify the **top 20% of tasks** that generate **80% of your income.**

◈ Eliminate or delegate **low-impact tasks.**

◈ Spend more time on **wealth-generating activities** like investing, networking, and creating passive income streams.

◈ **Example:** Instead of answering emails all day, a millionaire might:

◈ Spend an hour investing in real estate.

◈ Hire an assistant for admin work.

◈ Create content that generates **passive income.**

3. Millionaire Time Blocking: The 3-Hour Focus Rule

Most people waste hours multitasking. Millionaires **time-block their day** into focused **high-value work sessions.**

◈ **Step 1:** Identify 3 **money-generating** tasks.
◈ **Step 2:** Block 3 hours **for deep, focused work.**
◈ **Step 3:** Eliminate distractions (phone on silent, no social media).

◈ **Example:** Instead of checking Instagram every 10 minutes, a millionaire might use **3 focused hours to:**
◈ Write a sales page that generates $50,000.
◈ Research investment opportunities.
◈ Build a digital product that sells passively.

4. Millionaires Buy Back Their Time

Millionaires **don't do everything themselves**—they hire and delegate so they can focus on **high-value tasks.**

◈ **Examples of Buying Back Time:**
◈ Hiring a virtual assistant for **emails and admin tasks.**
◈ Using an accountant for **taxes and financial planning.**
◈ Investing in software that **automates repetitive work.**

By **outsourcing low-value tasks,** millionaires **free up time** to focus on making **high-level financial decisions.**

How Millionaires Manage Their Money

Millionaires don't just **earn** a lot—they **keep, grow, and protect** their wealth through smart money habits.

1. Pay Yourself First (The Wealth Rule)

The **#1 financial rule of millionaires:** Before spending on **anything**, they put a percentage of income into **investments.**

◈ **How to apply it:**

◈ Every time you earn money, **automatically save & invest 20-50%** before paying bills.

◈ Set up an **automatic transfer** into investment accounts.

◈ Treat saving **like a mandatory expense.**

◈ **Example:** If a millionaire makes $100,000, they might:

◈ Invest **$30,000 in stocks and real estate.**

◈ Save **$20,000 in an emergency fund.**

◈ Spend the rest **on lifestyle and expenses.**

2. The 50/30/20 Millionaire Budget

Unlike the average person, millionaires allocate their money with **purpose.**

◈ **50% - Wealth Growth** (Investments, real estate, business growth).

◈ **30% - Lifestyle** (Travel, fun, family).

◈ **20% - Safety Net** (Savings, emergency fund, insurance).

Most people do the opposite—they **spend first and save later.** Millionaires flip the formula: **invest first, enjoy later.**

3. The Golden Rule of Wealth: Assets Over Liabilities

Poor people buy luxuries first.

Millionaires buy assets first.

◈ **Example:**

◈ Poor mindset: Buying a new car (depreciating asset).

◈ Wealthy mindset: Buying an investment property that pays for the car.

◈ **How to apply it:**

◈ Before making a major purchase, ask: **"Will this make me more money in the future?"**

◈ Focus on buying **income-producing assets** before luxury items.

Powerful Investment Strategies for Generational Wealth

Millionaires don't just think about **today's money**—they build wealth that lasts **for generations.**

1. The Millionaire Investment Triangle: Stocks, Real Estate, and Business

Most wealthy people build their portfolio using these **three pillars of wealth:**

◈ **Stocks & Index Funds** (long-term growth).
◈ **Real Estate** (passive income & appreciation).
◈ **Businesses & Digital Assets** (cash flow & scalability).

◈ **How to start:**
◈ **Invest in stocks:** Buy ETFs or index funds (like the S&P 500).
◈ **Buy real estate:** Start with rental properties or REITs (Real Estate Investment Trusts).
◈ **Build a business:** Sell a product, service, or create passive income streams.

2. The Power of Compound Interest: Grow Money Automatically

Millionaires **use compound interest** to grow wealth over time.

◈ **Example:**
If you invest **$500/month** into a fund with **10% annual return**, in **30 years**, you'd have:
◈ **$1,000,000+**

◈ **How to start:**
◈ Open a **brokerage account (like Vanguard, Fidelity, or Robinhood).**
◈ Invest **monthly in index funds or dividend stocks.**
◈ Let your money **grow passively over time.**

3. Passive Income: The Key to Financial Freedom

Millionaires **don't rely on one income source**—they create **multiple streams** of income that pay them **passively.**

◈ **Best Passive Income Ideas:**

◈ **Rental properties** (Airbnb, long-term leases).
◈ **Dividend stocks** (paying consistent income).
◈ **Online businesses** (selling digital products, memberships).

◈ **How to start:**

◈ Choose **one passive income idea** to build over the next 6 months.
◈ Focus on **systems** that make money without needing daily work.

Final Thoughts: Becoming a Millionaire in Mindset and Money

Millionaires don't just **make money**—they manage time and wealth strategically. By **optimizing time, controlling spending, and investing wisely**, you will create financial freedom for yourself and **future generations.**

◈ **Your next action steps:**

◈ **Track your time** for a week—eliminate low-value tasks.
◈ **Automate savings & investments** before spending.
◈ **Choose an investment strategy** (stocks, real estate, business) and take action.

Your wealth journey **starts today. The sooner you start managing time and money like a millionaire, the sooner you become one.** ◈

Chapter 5: Creating Multiple Streams of Passive Income

How to Build Passive Income and Achieve True Financial Freedom!

Financial freedom isn't just about making money—it's about creating *income that flows to you whether you work or not.* The wealthiest people don't rely on a single source of income. Instead, they build **multiple streams of passive income**, ensuring they are financially secure no matter what happens in the economy.

In this chapter, we'll dive deep into **how to build multiple streams of passive income**, the best passive income strategies, and how to structure your financial life so that you never have to worry about money again. By implementing these principles, you'll be able to generate wealth *automatically*, giving you the freedom to live life on your own terms.

What is Passive Income?

Passive income is money you earn with little to no ongoing effort after the initial setup. Unlike traditional income where you trade time for money, passive income continues to flow even when you're sleeping, traveling, or focusing on other projects.

◈ Two Types of Income:

- **Active Income:** Requires **continuous effort** (e.g., a 9-to-5 job, freelancing).
- **Passive Income:** Earned **automatically** after an initial setup (e.g., investments, digital products, rental income).

Passive income **multiplies your earning potential** by detaching your time from your income. This is the key to **true financial freedom**—the ability to live life without depending on a paycheck.

The Power of Multiple Streams of Income

Most millionaires have **at least 7 income streams**—if one dries up, they still have others bringing in cash.

◈ **Why You Need Multiple Income Streams:** ◈ Increases financial stability—no reliance on a single job.

◈ Provides **security** during economic downturns.

◈ Allows you to **build wealth faster** and retire early.

◈ Creates **more freedom** to pursue your passions.

Now, let's explore the **best ways to create passive income** and build a financial system that works *for you*.

Top Passive Income Streams to Build Wealth

1. Investing in Stocks and Dividends (The Automatic Wealth Generator)

Investing is one of the easiest ways to **grow money passively**. By putting your money into stocks, bonds, and index funds, you let compound interest work its magic.

◈ **Best Stock Investment Strategies:**

◈ **Dividend Stocks:** Companies that pay you **regular cash dividends** (e.g., Coca-Cola, Apple, AT&T).

◈ **Index Funds & ETFs:** Low-risk funds that track the market (e.g., S&P 500).

◈ **Real Estate Investment Trusts (REITs):** Invest in real estate *without* buying property.

◈ **Example of Passive Growth:**

If you invest **$500/month in an S&P 500 index fund**, in **30 years** at a **10% return**, you'd have **$1,000,000+.**

◈ **How to Start:**

1. Open a **brokerage account** (Vanguard, Fidelity, Robinhood).
2. Start with **index funds and dividend stocks.**
3. Set up **automatic investments** each month.

Your money will grow even if you never touch it! ◈

2. Rental Real Estate (Build Wealth While You Sleep)

Owning rental properties is one of the most **stable and proven** ways to build long-term wealth.

⍰ **Best Rental Strategies:**

⍰ **Long-Term Rentals:** Buy property and rent it out for steady cash flow.

⍰ **Short-Term Rentals (Airbnb):** Higher profits but more management.

⍰ **REITs (No Property Needed):** Invest in real estate through the stock market.

⍰ **Example:**

If you own a property that rents for **$1,500/month** and expenses are **$800/month**, you pocket **$700/month in passive income.** Multiply this across **several properties**, and you've built a *money-printing machine*.

⍰ **How to Start:**

1. **Save for a down payment** or partner with an investor.
2. Buy property in **high-rental-demand areas**.
3. Hire a **property manager** for hands-off income.

Real estate creates generational wealth that lasts forever! ⍰

3. Selling Digital Products (Earn Forever with No Extra Work)

Creating **digital assets** allows you to earn **passive income with zero overhead costs.**

◈ **Best Digital Products to Sell:**

◈ **eBooks:** Sell on Amazon, Gumroad, or your website.

◈ **Online Courses:** Teach a skill once—sell it forever.

◈ **Printables & Templates:** Designs, planners, worksheets.

◈ **Stock Photos & Videos:** Upload to sites like Shutterstock.

◈ **Example:**

If you create an **ebook that sells for $20** and sell **50 copies per month**, that's an easy **$1,000/month** in passive income.

◈ **How to Start:**

1. Identify a **profitable niche**.
2. Create a **simple product** (ebook, template, course).
3. Sell it on platforms like **Amazon, Etsy, Gumroad, Teachable**.

Once created, digital products generate cash forever! ◈

4. Affiliate Marketing (Get Paid for Referrals)

Affiliate marketing is **one of the fastest ways** to make money online **passively**.

◈ **How It Works:**

◈ You **recommend products** and earn a commission when someone buys through your link.

◈ No need to create your own product—just promote existing ones.

◈ **Example:**

If you promote a **$100 product** with a **30% commission** and **10 people buy per month**, that's **$300/month** for *zero extra work!*

◈ **How to Start:**

1. Join **affiliate programs** (Amazon Associates, ClickBank, ShareASale).
2. Share links in a **blog, YouTube, or social media.**
3. Earn money whenever someone buys!

Affiliate marketing lets you profit from other people's products! ◈

5. Automated Businesses (Passive Income on Autopilot)

Instead of working a job, **own a system that makes money for you**.

◈ **Best Automated Business Models:**

◈ **Dropshipping:** Sell products online without inventory.
◈ **Amazon FBA:** Sell on Amazon—they handle shipping.
◈ **Subscription Services:** Membership sites, paid communities.

◈ **Example:**

If you run an **automated dropshipping store** and make **$5,000/ month**, but only **work 2 hours per week**, you're earning passive income!

◈ **How to Start:**

1. Pick a **business model** (dropshipping, print-on-demand).
2. Automate fulfillment using platforms like **Shopify, Amazon, Printful.**
3. Scale with **ads and organic traffic.**

Set up the system once—earn forever! ◈

How to Achieve True Financial Freedom

Creating multiple passive income streams is **only part of the equation**—you must also **structure your finances** for long-term wealth.

◈ **Follow the 70/30 Wealth Rule:**

◈ **70% of passive income reinvested** (stocks, real estate).

◈ **30% used for lifestyle and enjoyment.**

◈ **Focus on Scalable Income Streams:**

◈ Choose **income sources that grow over time** (investing, digital assets).

◈ Eliminate **low-value tasks** to free up time for higher-earning activities.

◈ **Set Long-Term Goals for Passive Income Growth:**

◈ Aim for **$1,000/month in passive income within a year.**

◈ Scale to **$10,000/month within 3-5 years.**

The goal is to reach a point where your **passive income covers all expenses**, meaning you **never have to work again unless you want to.**

Final Thoughts: Your Path to Financial Freedom Starts Now!

◈ **Your Next Steps:**

◈ Choose **one passive income stream** and start building it today.

◈ Set a **financial freedom goal** ($5,000/month in passive income).

◈ Automate and scale your wealth-building strategies.

By taking action **now**, you'll create a life where **money flows effortlessly, and financial stress disappears forever.** ◈

Chapter 6: Digital Real Estate: The New Gold Rush

Mastering Wealth Psychology—How to Think Like a Billionaire!

We are living in the **golden era of digital wealth creation.** Just as physical real estate has been the foundation of generational wealth for centuries, a new form of **real estate** has emerged in the digital world—one that allows you to own valuable online assets that generate income **24/7, with little overhead and infinite scalability.**

This is **Digital Real Estate**—the new gold rush of the modern economy.

In this chapter, we'll explore:

◈ What **digital real estate** is and why it's the **most lucrative investment** of the decade.

◈ How to acquire, build, and profit from **digital properties**.

◈ The **psychology of billionaires** and how they leverage **online assets** to create empires.

By the end of this chapter, you'll understand how to **invest in and control digital real estate**, setting yourself up for **limitless financial freedom and long-term wealth.**

What is Digital Real Estate?

Just like **physical real estate**, digital real estate consists of **assets you own online** that appreciate in value, generate passive income, and can be bought, sold, or rented.

🔷 **Examples of Digital Real Estate:**

🔷 Websites & Blogs (Ad revenue, affiliate marketing)
🔷 Domain Names (Flipping valuable domains)
🔷 YouTube Channels (AdSense, sponsorships)
🔷 Social Media Pages (Brand deals, advertising)
🔷 eCommerce Stores (Shopify, Amazon FBA)
🔷 Email Lists & Newsletters (Direct monetization)
🔷 NFTs & Metaverse Land (Virtual property investments)

Owning digital real estate is like **owning rental properties**—but instead of tenants paying rent, your digital assets generate revenue from **ads, sales, subscriptions, or traffic.**

Why Digital Real Estate is the New Gold Rush

1. Low Investment, High Returns

Unlike physical real estate, which requires **hundreds of thousands in capital**, digital real estate can be built with **as little as $10-$100** and scale to **millions.**

◈ **Example:**

- A **$10 domain name** can turn into a **$10,000+ asset** if it ranks on Google and generates ad revenue.
- A **$50 WordPress site** can make **$5,000/month** in passive income with affiliate marketing.

2. Infinite Scalability & Automation

Digital real estate is **not limited by geography** or physical space—it can reach **millions of people worldwide.** Once set up, **it runs on autopilot** with minimal effort.

◈ **Example:**

A **blog that ranks on Google** can bring **consistent traffic and sales** without extra work, just like a **rental property generating rent every month.**

3. High Demand & Appreciation

Just as physical properties increase in value, **so does digital real estate.**

- Websites that gain **more traffic become more valuable.**
- Social media pages with **huge followings can sell for six-figure sums.**
- Rare domain names get bought for **millions of dollars.**

◈ **Example:** In 2010, **Cars.com** sold for **$872 million.**

4. Multiple Income Streams from One Asset

Unlike physical property, which typically generates **one stream of rental income**, digital properties can make money in **several ways** simultaneously.

◈ **Example: A Blog Can Earn From:**
◈ Display Ads (Google AdSense, Mediavine)
◈ Affiliate Marketing (Amazon, ClickBank, ShareASale)
◈ Sponsored Content (Brands pay for promotions)
◈ Digital Products (eBooks, online courses)

A **single digital asset** can generate **multiple streams of income**, compounding wealth over time.

How to Invest in Digital Real Estate

There are **two main ways** to acquire digital assets:

1. Buy an Existing Digital Property (Fast Track to Wealth)

◈ **Purchase an already profitable website, blog, or social media account.**

◈ Improve monetization and increase revenue.

◈ Sell it later for **10x or more the original price.**

◈ **Best Platforms to Buy Digital Assets:**

- **Flippa.com** (Buy/Sell websites, blogs, eCommerce stores)
- **EmpireFlippers.com** (High-end online businesses)
- **MotionInvest.com** (Niche content websites)

◈ **Example:** A website making **$1,000/month** in passive income can be bought for **$30,000** and flipped for **$100,000+** after scaling.

2. Build a Digital Property from Scratch (Long-Term Growth)
◈ Start a **blog, YouTube channel, eCommerce store, or newsletter.**
◈ Grow traffic and build an audience.
◈ Monetize through **ads, sales, and sponsorships.**
◈ **Example:**

- A blog started today can make **$5,000+/month** in **2 years** with steady growth.
- A YouTube channel can generate **six-figure passive income** with viral content.

Billionaires don't wait for opportunities—they build them. Digital real estate is your chance to own **a piece of the internet's wealth.**

How Billionaires Think About Digital Real Estate

To truly **dominate the digital real estate game**, you must **think like a billionaire**. Here's the mindset shift:

1. Control Assets, Not Just Income

◈ **Poor mindset:** Work for money, spend it all.

◈ **Wealthy mindset:** Own digital assets that make money for you.

◈ **Example:** Instead of just making YouTube videos, **own the YouTube channel.** Instead of promoting products, **own the online store.**

2. Leverage Other People's Work (OPW) & Systems (OPS)

Billionaires **don't work harder—they build systems that work for them.**

◈ **Example:**

◈ Use **AI & automation** to run blogs, eCommerce stores, and email lists.

◈ Hire **content creators** to grow social media accounts.

◈ **Outsource** digital product creation to freelancers.

Once a digital asset is built, it should generate income without constant effort.

3. Scale and Multiply Profits

A billionaire's goal isn't just **one successful asset**—it's **10x-ing wealth by reinvesting in more assets.**

◈ **Example:**

- Use revenue from a **blog to buy a profitable website.**
- Use **eCommerce profits to invest in real estate.**
- Sell one **successful digital business** and start a bigger one.

Billionaires **use one success to fund the next, compounding wealth exponentially.**

Your Roadmap to Building Digital Real Estate Wealth

◈ **Step 1: Pick a Digital Real Estate Asset**

◈ Blog, YouTube, eCommerce, newsletter, domain flipping.

◈ **Step 2: Build or Buy an Asset**

◈ Start from scratch **or buy an existing site.**

◈ **Step 3: Scale & Monetize**

◈ Add **ads, affiliate links, digital products, and services.**

◈ **Step 4: Automate & Outsource**

◈ Use **AI, freelancers, and automation tools.**

◈ **Step 5: Reinvest & Expand**

◈ Buy more digital properties, reinvest earnings, and **repeat the cycle.**

Final Thoughts: The Future of Digital Wealth

◈ *The internet is the greatest wealth-creation tool in history.*

◈ *Owning digital real estate is like owning prime land—except there are no limits!*

Your Next Steps:

◈ **Pick a digital real estate model** and start today.

◈ **Think like a billionaire—control assets, not just income.**

◈ **Leverage automation and reinvest in more properties.**

By following this blueprint, **you won't just make money—you'll create unstoppable generational wealth.** ◈

Chapter 7: The Hidden Power of Compound Wealth

The Wealth Matrix—Mastering the Art of Financial Control

Wealth isn't just built through earning—it's **compounded over time** through strategic financial control. While many people believe that becoming rich requires a massive income, the truth is that **long-term wealth is a result of leveraging compound growth, smart investments, and financial discipline.**

The world's richest individuals understand **The Wealth Matrix**, a system that ensures they never run out of money and their wealth continues to grow even while they sleep.

In this chapter, you'll learn:

◈ The **hidden power of compound wealth** and how to make your money grow automatically.

◈ How to **master financial control** using The Wealth Matrix.

◈ The **systems billionaires use** to ensure they never go broke.

By mastering **compound wealth**, you'll create a self-sustaining financial empire that provides **financial security, freedom, and generational wealth.**

What is Compound Wealth?

Compound wealth is the ability of money to grow exponentially over time when **invested correctly**. It follows the principle of **compound interest**, which Albert Einstein famously called:

"The eighth wonder of the world. He who understands it, earns it. He who doesn't, pays it."

◈ **How It Works:**

- Money earns **interest or returns.**
- Those returns get reinvested.
- Over time, **returns earn returns**, and the money grows exponentially.

◈ **Example:**

If you invest **$10,000** at **10% annual growth**, after:

◈ **1 year:** $11,000

◈ **5 years:** $16,105

◈ **10 years:** $25,937

◈ **30 years: $174,494** ◈

The key is **starting early and reinvesting consistently.**

The Wealth Matrix: Mastering Financial Control

Wealth isn't just about **earning—it's about controlling money, directing it strategically, and making it work for you.**

The **Wealth Matrix** is a **financial system** that ensures you:

◈ Always **have money flowing in.**
◈ Keep **expenses in check.**
◈ Grow your wealth **without active work.**

The 4 Pillars of the Wealth Matrix

1. The Income Flow Pillar: Multiple Streams of Wealth

The wealthy **never rely on one source of income.** Instead, they create **multiple revenue streams** so they are financially secure no matter what happens.

◈ **Income Sources to Build:**

◈ **Active Income** (job, business, consulting)
◈ **Passive Income** (investments, digital products, real estate)
◈ **Scalable Income** (courses, affiliate marketing, royalties)

◈ **Action Step:** List **3 passive income streams** you can start building today.

2. The Wealth Acceleration Pillar: High-Yield Investments

Billionaires **don't just save money—they multiply it** by investing in **assets that compound over time.**

◈ **Best Compound Wealth Investments:**

◈ **Stocks & Index Funds** (long-term growth)
◈ **Dividend Stocks** (earn passive cash flow)
◈ **Real Estate** (rental income & appreciation)
◈ **Businesses & Digital Assets** (online stores, blogs)

◈ **Action Step:** Start investing **$100 per month** in a high-growth asset (index fund, stock portfolio).

3. The Protection Pillar: Never Go Broke Again

Wealthy individuals **protect** their money so they never lose everything.

◈ **How to Secure Your Finances:**

◈ **Emergency Fund** (6-12 months of expenses)
◈ **Insurance & Asset Protection** (real estate, trusts)
◈ **Low-Risk Investments** (bonds, real estate syndicates)

◈ **Action Step:** Open a **separate savings account** and set up automatic transfers for your **financial safety net.**

4. The Wealth Freedom Pillar: Make Money Work for You

The ultimate goal of wealth-building is **financial freedom**, where your **investments generate enough passive income to cover all expenses.**

◈ **Formula for Financial Freedom:**

◈ **Total Monthly Passive Income > Total Monthly Expenses**

◈ **Example:**

- **Expenses:** $5,000/month
- **Passive Income:** $6,000/month
- ◈ *You're financially free!*

◈ **Action Step:** Calculate how much **passive income you need to cover your expenses** and start working towards it.

The 10-Year Billionaire Plan (How to Build Compound Wealth Fast)

◈ *Most people overestimate what they can do in a year and underestimate what they can do in a decade.*

Use this **step-by-step plan** to build financial independence in the next **10 years.**

Year 1-2: Build Your Income Base

◈ Develop **high-income skills** (sales, investing, copywriting).
◈ Start **one passive income stream** (blog, YouTube, eCommerce).
◈ Invest **10-20% of earnings** into compound wealth assets.

Year 3-5: Expand and Multiply

◈ Grow to **3-5 income streams.**
◈ Buy **real estate or digital assets.**
◈ Increase **investment contributions.**
◈ Reinvest profits to **scale wealth.**

Year 6-10: Achieve Financial Freedom

◈ Passive income exceeds expenses.
◈ Automate finances with **systems & outsourcing.**
◈ Scale wealth into **generational investments.**

◈ **Action Step:** Create a **10-year financial roadmap** using this plan.

The Billionaire Mindset: Thinking Long-Term Like the Wealthy

The biggest difference between **rich and poor people** isn't their **money**—it's their **mindset and time horizon.**

◈ **Billionaires Think in Decades, Not Days**

◈ *Poor mindset:* "How can I make money today?"

◈ *Wealth mindset:* "How can I build wealth that lasts 100 years?"

◈ **Billionaires Focus on Systems, Not Shortcuts**

◈ *Poor mindset:* "What's the fastest way to get rich?"

◈ *Wealth mindset:* "What system can I create that prints money forever?"

◈ **Billionaires Invest, Not Just Save**

◈ *Poor mindset:* "I need to save money."

◈ *Wealth mindset:* "I need to multiply money."

◈ **Billionaires Own Assets, Not Just Income**

◈ *Poor mindset:* "I need a higher salary."

◈ *Wealth mindset:* "I need to own businesses, real estate, and stocks."

◈ **Action Step:** Shift your mindset from **instant gratification** to **long-term wealth-building.**

Final Thoughts: Your Wealth Compound Blueprint

To master **The Wealth Matrix**, follow these key principles:

◈ **Own assets** that generate money **without trading time.**

◈ **Invest early and let compound interest do the work.**

◈ **Diversify income streams** to create financial security.

◈ **Think like a billionaire—focus on long-term wealth.**

◈ **Your Next Steps:**

◈ Choose **one passive income stream** and start building today.

◈ Invest in **one compound asset** (stocks, real estate, business).

◈ Plan your **10-year wealth strategy** and start executing.

The sooner you start, the sooner you'll achieve financial freedom. Don't wait—take action now and let your wealth compound for decades to come!

Chapter 8: The Law of Reciprocity in Business and Finance

The Financial Independence Formula—Escaping the 9-to-5 Forever

One of the most **overlooked yet powerful** principles in business and finance is **The Law of Reciprocity**—the universal rule that states: *"The more value you give, the more wealth you attract."*

Successful entrepreneurs, investors, and billionaires don't just focus on **making money**—they focus on **providing massive value** to others. In return, they receive wealth, opportunities, and influence far beyond what they initially gave.

In this chapter, we'll explore:

◈ How the **Law of Reciprocity** drives business success and financial growth.

◈ Why **giving value first** is the secret to escaping the 9-to-5 forever.

◈ The **Financial Independence Formula** that allows you to live on your own terms.

By the end of this chapter, you'll understand how to **leverage reciprocity to create financial abundance** while building relationships that open doors to unlimited success.

The Law of Reciprocity: The Secret to Wealth Creation

The Law of Reciprocity is a fundamental human principle:

"When you give freely, people feel a natural obligation to return the favor—sometimes in ways that far exceed what you originally gave."

◈ **Examples in Business & Finance:**

◈ A **business gives away free value** (content, samples, insights), and in return, people become paying customers.

◈ A **networker helps others first**, and in return, they receive job offers, business deals, or funding.

◈ An **investor provides capital**, and in return, they earn **exponential returns** over time.

This is why **billionaires give before they receive**—they understand that **money follows value, not the other way around.**

How Reciprocity Works in Wealth Building

Reciprocity creates a **cycle of abundance**—the more value you provide, the more financial opportunities flow to you.

1. The Value-First Mindset: Give Before You Expect to Receive

Most people approach money with a **take-first** mindset:

⟐ *"How can I make money today?"*
⟐ *"What can I get from this person?"*

But **wealthy individuals operate differently**:

⟐ *"How can I provide value today?"*
⟐ *"What can I offer that will benefit others?"*

⟐ **Examples of Giving Value First:**

⟐ **Content Creators:** Give free educational content → Build trust → Monetize through products.
⟐ **Investors:** Provide funding to startups → Earn long-term equity.
⟐ **Businesses:** Offer free trials → Gain lifelong customers.

⟐ **Action Step:** Identify **one way you can give value today** (free content, insights, help, networking).

2. Building Wealth Through Relationship Capital

Money doesn't just come from **transactions**—it comes from **relationships.** The wealthiest people don't just focus on making sales; they focus on **building connections that create lifelong opportunities.**

◈ **Why Relationship Capital Matters:**

◈ Your **net worth** is tied to your **network**.
◈ The **stronger your connections**, the more wealth flows to you.
◈ Trust opens **doors to partnerships, investments, and collaborations.**

◈ **How to Apply This:**

1. **Help someone in your industry without asking for anything in return.**
2. **Make meaningful connections**—not just sales-driven interactions.
3. **Offer introductions** between people who can help each other.

◈ **Action Step:** Find **one person today** who could benefit from your expertise, insight, or network.

3. Business Reciprocity: Why Giving Free Value Leads to Exponential Income

The best businesses **don't sell first—they serve first.**

◈ **Example:**

- Google gives **free search services** → Earns billions from ads.
- Amazon offers **free shipping (Prime)** → Customers buy more.
- Tesla lets people test-drive cars **for free** → More sales.

The more value you provide upfront, the more trust and sales you generate later.

◈ **Action Step:** Create a **"give first" strategy** in your business or personal brand (free guides, content, advice, consultations).

The Financial Independence Formula: Escaping the 9-to-5 Forever

If you want to **quit your job and achieve financial freedom**, you must **shift from earning money actively to earning passively**.

Step 1: Understand the Financial Independence Formula

To escape the 9-to-5, you need **one simple formula**:

◈ **Total Monthly Passive Income > Total Monthly Expenses**

◈ **Example:**

- If your total monthly expenses = **$5,000**
- Your passive income = **$6,000**
- ◈ *You're financially free!*

◈ **Action Step:** Calculate your **financial freedom number**—how much passive income you need to cover your living expenses.

Step 2: Create Multiple Passive Income Streams

Relying on a **single income source** keeps you trapped in a job. The wealthy **diversify their income.**

◈ **Best Passive Income Streams:**

◈ **Dividend Stocks** (Cash flow from investments)
◈ **Rental Real Estate** (Long-term wealth growth)
◈ **Digital Products** (Courses, eBooks, memberships)
◈ **Affiliate Marketing** (Earn from promoting products)
◈ **Automated Online Businesses** (Dropshipping, print-on-demand)

◈ **Action Step:** Choose **one passive income idea** and start building it today.

Step 3: Automate & Scale Your Wealth

Financial independence isn't about **working harder**—it's about **building systems that make money for you.**

◈ **How to Automate Wealth:**

◈ **Set up automatic investments** into stocks & assets.

◈ **Create passive income systems** that run without your input.

◈ **Leverage outsourcing** to free up your time.

◈ **Action Step:** Automate at least **one financial process** this week (investment contributions, auto-savings, outsourcing).

Step 4: Live on Less Than You Earn & Reinvest the Difference

If you want to quit your job **faster**, you need to **scale passive income while reducing unnecessary expenses.**

◈ **How to Speed Up Financial Freedom:**

◈ Cut **non-essential expenses** and redirect that money into investments.

◈ Reinvest **100% of passive income** into more wealth-generating assets.

◈ Build a **1-3 year runway** of savings to cover expenses if needed.

◈ **Action Step:** Identify **3 expenses to eliminate today** and reinvest that money into wealth-building.

Final Thoughts: How Reciprocity Leads to Financial Freedom

The **Law of Reciprocity** isn't just about **giving—it's about receiving opportunities, wealth, and financial independence in return.**

Your 3-Part Wealth Strategy:

◈ **Give first, receive later** (trust builds wealth).

◈ **Build multiple income streams** (quit the 9-to-5 faster).

◈ **Automate your financial success** (set systems to work for you).

◈ **Your Next Steps:**

◈ **Find one way to provide value** to your network or audience today.

◈ **Create one passive income stream** and work toward your financial freedom number.

◈ **Automate wealth-building systems** and scale your earnings over time.

By applying **The Law of Reciprocity**, you'll unlock **financial independence faster than you ever imagined.** ◈

Chapter 9: Turning Setbacks into Financial Breakthroughs

The Money Flow Code—How to Control and Direct Wealth Like a Financial Mastermind

Every successful entrepreneur, investor, and self-made millionaire has faced **financial setbacks**. But what separates the wealthy from the struggling is their **ability to turn setbacks into breakthroughs**.

Setbacks—whether they come in the form of **business failures, bad investments, job losses, or economic downturns**—are not the end of the road. Instead, they are **hidden opportunities for massive financial growth.**

In this chapter, we'll explore:

◈ How to **reframe financial setbacks** into powerful learning experiences.

◈ The **Money Flow Code**—a strategic system to control, allocate, and grow wealth.

◈ How to **recover from financial losses** and come back stronger.

By mastering **the psychology of financial resilience and the strategic movement of money**, you will transform every financial challenge into **a stepping stone to wealth mastery.**

Why Financial Setbacks Are Inevitable (and Necessary)

Many people believe that **financial success is a straight upward path**—but this is **a myth.**

◈ **The Truth About Wealth Creation:**

◈ Every millionaire has **lost money** before making millions.
◈ Setbacks **test and refine** your ability to handle wealth.
◈ The wealthiest individuals see **losses as tuition for financial mastery.**

◈ **Examples of Financial Comebacks:**

- **Elon Musk** was **$180 million in debt** after investing all his PayPal earnings into Tesla & SpaceX—today, he is one of the richest men alive.
- **Walt Disney** went bankrupt before building the Disney empire.
- **Steve Jobs** was fired from Apple before returning and making it a trillion-dollar company.

◈ **Lesson: Setbacks are not failures—they are feedback.**

◈ **Action Step:** Write down **one financial setback** you've experienced and identify **what you learned from it.**

The 3-Step Formula for Turning Setbacks into Financial Breakthroughs

Every **financial setback contains the seed of a future breakthrough**—but only if you know how to extract it.

Step 1: Reframe the Setback as an Opportunity

The **biggest mistake** people make when facing a financial loss is **falling into victim mode.** Instead, you must **train your brain to see opportunity in every challenge.**

◈ **Reframing Examples:**

◈ *"I lost my job—I'm doomed."*

◈ *"This is my chance to start my own business and take control of my income."*

◈ *"I lost money in the stock market—I should stop investing."*

◈ *"This loss is teaching me better risk management for future bigger investments."*

◈ **Action Step:** Write down **one positive lesson** you can take from a financial setback.

Step 2: Apply the Wealth Adaptation Principle

The wealthiest individuals **don't dwell on losses**—they **adapt quickly and move forward.**

◈ **The Wealth Adaptation Principle:**

◈ **Analyze** what went wrong.

◈ **Adjust your financial strategy.**

◈ **Take action again with improved knowledge.**

◈ **Example:** If you lost money in real estate, instead of quitting:

◈ Study **what went wrong** (bad location, wrong timing, overpaying).

◈ Adjust your **investment criteria** (better market research, lower risk deals).

◈ Take action again **with improved strategies.**

◈ **Action Step:** Identify **one financial mistake** you made and create a plan to improve your decision-making next time.

Step 3: Shift from Scarcity to Wealth Expansion Mode

Most people **retreat into financial fear** after a loss—but this is the **worst thing you can do.** Instead of contracting, you must **expand your mindset and wealth strategies.**

◈ **The Shift from Scarcity to Wealth Expansion:**

◈ **Scarcity Thinking:** "I need to save everything and avoid risks."

◈ **Wealth Thinking:** "I need to invest wisely and create multiple income streams."

◈ **Example:**

After losing money in a business, instead of stopping:

◈ Learn **new monetization strategies.**

◈ Expand into **digital products, coaching, or investments.**

◈ Network with **successful people who have recovered from losses.**

◈ **Action Step:** Identify **one area where you've been thinking too small** and commit to expanding your wealth strategy.

The Money Flow Code—How to Control and Direct Wealth Like a Financial Mastermind

The **Money Flow Code** is a system designed to **strategically allocate money** in a way that maximizes financial security, growth, and freedom.

The key to financial success isn't just **earning more**—it's knowing **where to put your money** so it works for you.

◈ **How the Wealthy Manage Money:**

◈ They **control cash flow**—money never just "sits" in a bank account.

◈ They **direct money into wealth-building activities.**

◈ They **automate money movement** to eliminate bad financial habits.

The 5-Part Money Flow Code

1. The Wealth Acceleration Bucket (40%)

◈ **Purpose:** Grow wealth through high-return investments.

◈ **Stocks & Index Funds** (S&P 500, dividend stocks).
◈ **Real Estate & REITs** (rental properties, real estate funds).
◈ **Crypto & Alternative Investments** (Bitcoin, Ethereum).
◈ **Online Businesses** (eCommerce, digital products, passive income streams).

◈ **Action Step:** Set up **automated monthly investments** into a wealth-growing asset.

2. The Cashflow Protection Bucket (30%)

◈ **Purpose:** Ensure financial security with emergency & safety funds.

◈ **Emergency Fund (6-12 months of expenses).**
◈ **Insurance** (health, life, income protection).
◈ **Low-Risk Investments** (bonds, fixed deposits).

◈ **Action Step:** Transfer at least **$500-$1,000 into an emergency fund today.**

3. The Wealth Reinforcement Bucket (10%)

◈ **Purpose:** Education & skill-building to increase earning potential.

◈ **High-income skills training** (sales, marketing, investing).
◈ **Books, courses, mentorships** for personal growth.
◈ **Networking & masterminds** to learn from successful people.

◈ **Action Step:** Invest in **one skill-building course or book** this month.

4. The Freedom Fund Bucket (10%)

◈ **Purpose:** Automate future financial independence.

◈ Invest in **long-term passive income assets**.

◈ Automate **retirement savings** (IRA, Roth IRA, 401k).

◈ Buy **cash-flowing businesses** (rental properties, online businesses).

◈ **Action Step:** Set up a **retirement account** and automate monthly contributions.

5. The Lifestyle & Giving Bucket (10%)

◈ **Purpose:** Enjoy life & practice generosity without guilt.

◈ Travel, experiences, personal luxuries.

◈ Charitable donations & supporting causes.

◈ Guilt-free spending within financial limits.

◈ **Action Step:** Set aside a **fixed percentage** for personal enjoyment.

Final Thoughts: How to Use Setbacks to Build Generational Wealth

◈ *The greatest financial breakthroughs come from mastering setbacks and directing money strategically.*

Your Money Flow Code Success Plan:

◈ **Reframe setbacks as stepping stones** to bigger opportunities.

◈ **Apply The Wealth Adaptation Principle**—analyze, adjust, and take action.

◈ **Control your money flow** using **The Money Flow Code.**

◈ **Your Next Steps:**

◈ Identify **one past financial setback** and extract **a powerful lesson.**

◈ Apply **The Money Flow Code** to **automate wealth growth.**

◈ Make **one bold financial move** today that aligns with long-term wealth building.

By mastering **setbacks and financial flow**, you will unlock **financial control and unlimited wealth-building potential.**

Chapter 10: Becoming an Unstoppable Money Magnet

The Infinite Leverage System—How to Use Other People's Money to Build Wealth Faster

Wealth is **not built in isolation**—it is built through **leveraging resources, capital, networks, and systems** that allow you to grow money exponentially. The secret of the rich isn't just that they have money—it's that they know **how to attract and multiply it at will.**

By the end of this chapter, you will understand:

◈ How to become a **money magnet** that effortlessly attracts wealth.

◈ The **Infinite Leverage System**—how to use other people's money, time, and skills to build wealth faster.

◈ The exact **mindset, habits, and systems** that turn you into a financial powerhouse.

This is the final step in your journey to **financial mastery, passive income, and unlimited wealth creation.** ◈

What Does It Mean to Be a Money Magnet?

A **money magnet** is someone who:

◈ Consistently **attracts financial opportunities, investments, and partnerships.**

◈ Makes money flow **to them effortlessly** instead of chasing it.

◈ Uses **leverage to multiply** their wealth instead of relying only on their own resources.

◈ **Key Difference Between Struggling & Wealthy People:**

◈ *Struggling people think money is scarce and hard to get.*

◈ *Wealthy people know that money is abundant and flows to those who create value and use leverage.*

◈ **Action Step:** Shift your mindset from **scarcity** (*"I need to work harder for money"*) to **abundance** (*"Money flows to me because I create value and use leverage."*)

The Infinite Leverage System—How to Use Other People's Money to Build Wealth Faster

The fastest way to wealth isn't by **saving money**—it's by **leveraging other people's money (OPM), time (OPT), skills (OPS), and systems (OPSy).**

◈ **What is Leverage?**

Leverage means using **outside resources to multiply wealth, speed up financial success, and reduce personal effort.**

◈ **4 Types of Infinite Leverage:**

1◈ **Other People's Money (OPM)**—Use loans, investor capital, and financing to acquire assets.

2◈ **Other People's Time (OPT)**—Delegate and hire so you can focus on **high-value activities.**

3◈ **Other People's Skills (OPS)**—Use **experts, freelancers, and employees** to execute work faster.

4◈ **Other People's Systems (OPSy)**—Use **automation, AI, and digital platforms** to scale income.

Let's break each one down.

1. Using Other People's Money (OPM) to Build Wealth Faster

Most people believe they must **save money for years** before they can invest. Wealthy individuals, on the other hand, **use other people's money** (banks, investors, loans) to acquire assets **faster**.

◈ **How the Rich Use OPM:**

◈ Real estate investors use **mortgages** to buy properties that generate rental income.

◈ Entrepreneurs get **business loans** or **investor funding** to launch companies.

◈ Stock market investors use **leverage (margin accounts)** to amplify returns.

◈ **Example:**

Instead of saving **$100,000 for 10 years** to buy a house in cash, a smart investor:

◈ Takes a **loan**, buys **5 rental properties**, and earns **passive income from tenants**.

◈ Uses **that cash flow** to pay off the loan and keep the profits.

◈ **Action Step:** Identify one way you can use **OPM** to accelerate your wealth-building (a business loan, real estate financing, or investor capital).

2. Using Other People's Time (OPT) to Work Less and Earn More

The wealthy don't do **everything themselves**—they **delegate** and use **teams** to scale their wealth.

◈ **OPT in Action:**

◈ **Entrepreneurs hire teams** to run businesses while they focus on strategy.

◈ **Real estate investors hire property managers** to handle tenants.

◈ **Influencers use video editors, social media managers, and assistants** to scale their brand.

◈ **How to Apply This:**

◈ If you have a business, **outsource repetitive work** so you can focus on **growth.**

◈ Use **virtual assistants** to manage administrative tasks.

◈ Hire **freelancers and automation tools** to multiply productivity.

◈ **Action Step:** Identify **one task** you can delegate today to **free up time for high-value wealth-building activities.**

3. Using Other People's Skills (OPS) to Create Multiple Income Streams

⯑ The wealthiest people don't need to be **experts at everything**—they surround themselves with **people who have specialized skills.**

⯑ **How to Leverage OPS:**

⯑ Instead of learning web design, hire a **web designer** to build your site.

⯑ Instead of mastering copywriting, hire a **freelance writer** to create content.

⯑ Instead of spending **years learning investing**, partner with **seasoned investors.**

⯑ **Action Step:** Write down **3 skills** you need to grow your income. Find experts to **help you scale faster.**

4. Using Other People's Systems (OPSy) to Automate Wealth

Billionaires don't **work harder**—they **build systems that generate wealth automatically.**

⯑ **Examples of OPSy in Action:**

⯑ **Automated Investing:** Use **Robo-advisors, auto-transfers, and passive ETFs.**

⯑ **Online Businesses:** Sell digital products that generate **passive sales.**

⯑ **Marketing Automation:** Use email sequences and AI to sell **while you sleep.**

⯑ **Action Step:** Set up **one financial automation today** (investment auto-deposit, automated email funnel, or AI tool).

Final Steps to Becoming an Unstoppable Money Magnet

Now that you understand **The Infinite Leverage System**, let's finalize your journey to financial freedom.

◈ **Step 1: Create a Magnetic Wealth Mindset**

◈ Stop **trading time for money**—focus on **building assets and systems.**

◈ Shift from **"I can't afford it"** to **"How can I create it?"**

◈ Replace **fear of risk** with **calculated investments.**

◈ **Action Step:** Write down **one limiting belief** about money and replace it with a **wealth-magnet belief.**

◈ **Step 2: Implement The Infinite Leverage System**

◈ Use **OPM** (loans, funding, investments) to buy wealth-building assets.

◈ Use **OPT** (employees, virtual assistants, freelancers) to scale income.

◈ Use **OPS** (experts, specialists) to build businesses faster.

◈ Use **OPSy** (automation tools, AI, online platforms) to generate passive income.

◈ **Action Step:** Pick **one leverage strategy** to start using today.

◈ **Step 3: Master the Money Flow Code**

◈ Direct your money into **assets, not liabilities.**

◈ Set up **automated investments.**

◈ Use **passive income streams** to cover living expenses.

◈ **Action Step:** Set up a **monthly automatic investment** in an **income-producing asset.**

Final Thoughts: You Are Now Financially Unstoppable

◈ **The secret to becoming a Money Magnet is simple:**

◈ **Provide massive value.**

◈ **Use leverage to multiply wealth.**

◈ **Automate, invest, and reinvest continuously.**

◈ **Your Next Steps:**

◈ Apply **one leverage strategy** today.

◈ Set a **clear financial freedom goal** ($10K/month passive income).

◈ Take **consistent action** every day to grow your **financial empire.**

By mastering **The Infinite Leverage System**, you will **never struggle for money again.** The **world is filled with opportunities**—and now, you have the **blueprint to attract wealth effortlessly.**

◈ *You are no longer just making money—you are becoming unstoppable.* ◈

Appendix A: Wealth-Building Exercises

This appendix contains **powerful, actionable wealth-building exercises** designed to help you solidify the principles covered in this book. Each exercise is crafted to **train your mind, enhance financial intelligence, and accelerate wealth accumulation.**

By consistently applying these exercises, you will **develop the mindset, habits, and financial strategies** necessary to create, sustain, and multiply wealth.

Section 1: Mastering the Wealth Mindset

Exercise 1: Identify and Replace Limiting Money Beliefs

Your **beliefs about money** shape your financial reality. If you hold negative beliefs, they will **block wealth from flowing to you.**

◈ **Step 1:** Write down the top **5 negative money beliefs** you hold.
◈ **Step 2:** Reframe each negative belief into an **empowering wealth belief.**

◈ **Example:**
◈ Negative: "Money is hard to make."
◈ Positive: "Money flows to me easily and effortlessly because I create value."

◈ **Action:** Repeat your new wealth beliefs **every morning and night for 30 days.**

Exercise 2: Train Your Brain to See Wealth Opportunities

Most people overlook financial opportunities because their **brain is trained to focus on lack.** This exercise will **retrain your Reticular Activating System (RAS)** to recognize **opportunities for income growth.**

◈ **Step 1:** Every day, write down **3 money-making opportunities** you notice (business ideas, investment opportunities, digital trends).

◈ **Step 2:** Pick **one opportunity each week** and research it further.

◈ **Action:** Commit to this exercise for **30 days** and track how your financial awareness expands.

Section 2: Mastering Money Flow and Control

Exercise 3: The Wealth Tracking Challenge

Wealthy individuals **track their money meticulously** because **what gets measured improves.**

◈ **Step 1:** Create a simple financial tracking sheet (or use an app like Mint, YNAB, or Personal Capital).

◈ **Step 2:** Track **every dollar you earn, spend, and invest** for the next **30 days.**

◈ **Key Insights to Look For:**

◈ Where are you **wasting money?**

◈ What **expenses can be redirected** toward investments?

◈ Are you **growing or shrinking your net worth?**

◈ **Action:** Set up a **monthly wealth review** to analyze your financial trends and make adjustments.

Exercise 4: The Automatic Wealth Flow System

Financially successful people **automate wealth-building** instead of relying on willpower.

◈ **Step 1:** Set up **automatic transfers** so that a percentage of every paycheck goes directly into:

◈ **Investments (stocks, real estate, crypto, business growth).**

◈ **Wealth security (savings, emergency fund, insurance).**

◈ **Personal development (books, courses, coaching).**

◈ **Action:** Set up at least **one automatic investment or savings transfer today.**

Section 3: Income Expansion Strategies

Exercise 5: The Multiple Income Stream Blueprint

Most millionaires have **at least 7 income streams.** This exercise helps you **map out your future income expansion.**

◈ **Step 1:** List **your current income sources.**

◈ **Step 2:** Identify **3 additional income streams** you can start building.

◈ **Step 3:** Create a **6-month action plan** to develop these streams.

◈ **Income Stream Ideas:**

◈ Digital products (eBooks, courses).

◈ Freelance or consulting work.

◈ Dividend stock investments.

◈ Rental properties.

◈ Affiliate marketing.

◈ **Action:** Take **one step today** toward building a new income stream.

Exercise 6: The 10X Income Growth Formula

To escape the 9-to-5, you must **increase your earning potential.**

◈ **Step 1:** Identify **one high-income skill** (copywriting, sales, investing, public speaking, digital marketing).

◈ **Step 2:** Invest in **mastering this skill** (courses, mentors, practice).

◈ **Step 3:** Use this skill to **increase your income by 10X.**

◈ **Action:** Find and enroll in **one course or mentorship** that will boost your income-generating skills.

Section 4: Leveraging Other People's Resources (The Infinite Leverage System)

Exercise 7: The OPM Wealth Acceleration Plan

Using **Other People's Money (OPM)** is the fastest way to build wealth.

◈ **Step 1:** Identify **one way you can use OPM** to invest (real estate financing, business loans, investor funding).

◈ **Step 2:** Research funding sources (banks, angel investors, venture capital, business credit lines).

◈ **Step 3:** Create a **funding plan** to acquire assets **without using your own money.**

◈ **Action:** Apply for at least **one funding opportunity** that aligns with your investment strategy.

Exercise 8: The OPT & OPS Delegation Strategy

Time is your **most valuable asset.** This exercise helps you **use Other People's Time (OPT) and Other People's Skills (OPS) to accelerate success.**

◈ **Step 1:** List **low-value tasks** you currently do that someone else could handle.

◈ **Step 2:** Identify **freelancers, virtual assistants, or automation tools** to delegate these tasks.

◈ **Step 3:** Focus your freed-up time on **high-value activities** like investing, networking, or business strategy.

◈ **Action:** Hire **one freelancer** or use **one automation tool** this week to optimize your time.

Section 5: Financial Freedom & Legacy Wealth

Exercise 9: The Financial Freedom Calculator

To achieve financial freedom, you must know **your exact freedom number.**

◈ **Step 1:** Calculate **your total monthly expenses.**
◈ **Step 2:** Multiply by 12 to get **annual financial needs.**
◈ **Step 3:** Identify **how much passive income** you need to cover your expenses.

◈ **Example:**
◈ Monthly expenses: **$5,000**
◈ Annual expenses: **$60,000**
◈ Passive income goal: **$60,000/year**

◈ **Action:** Set a **passive income goal** and create a **3-year plan** to reach it.

Exercise 10: The Legacy Wealth Plan

True wealth isn't just about **you**—it's about **generational impact.**

◈ **Step 1:** Define your **legacy wealth goals** (real estate empire, trust funds, generational businesses).
◈ **Step 2:** Start setting up **legacy investments** (life insurance, estate planning, generational wealth funds).
◈ **Step 3:** Document **your wealth-building strategies** to pass on to future generations.

◈ **Action:** Write a **Wealth Legacy Letter** detailing your financial principles, investment philosophy, and family wealth-building plan.

Final Thoughts: Transforming Wealth Knowledge into Action

Reading about wealth-building is **only valuable if you take action.**

◈ **Your Wealth Action Plan:**

◈ Pick **3 exercises** to implement this week.

◈ Track your progress **over the next 30 days.**

◈ Commit to making **wealth-building a lifelong habit.**

By consistently applying these exercises, you will **rewire your financial reality, attract limitless wealth, and achieve complete financial freedom.**

◈ *Your financial transformation starts now!* ◈

Message from the Author:

I hope you enjoyed this book, I love astrology and knew there was not a book such as this out on the shelf. I love metaphysical items as well. Please check out my other books:

-Life of Government Benefits

-My life of Hell

-My life with Hydrocephalus

-Red Sky

-World Domination:Woman's rule

-World Domination:Woman's Rule 2: The War

-Life and Banishment of Apophis: book 1

-The Kidney Friendly Diet

-The Ultimate Hemp Cookbook

-Creating a Dispensary(legally)

-Cleanliness throughout life: the importance of showering from childhood to adulthood.

-Strong Roots: The Risks of Overcoddling children

-Hemp Horoscopes: Cosmic Insights and Earthly Healing

- Celestial Hemp Navigating the Zodiac: Through the Green Cosmos

-Astrological Hemp: Aligning The Stars with Earth's Ancient Herb

-The Astrological Guide to Hemp: Stars, Signs, and Sacred Leaves

-Green Growth: Innovative Marketing Strategies for your Hemp Products and Dispensary

-Cosmic Cannabis

-Astrological Munchies

-Henry The Hemp

-Zodiacal Roots: The Astrological Soul Of Hemp

- **Green Constellations: Intersection of Hemp and Zodiac**

-Hemp in The Houses: An astrological Adventure Through The Cannabis Galaxy

-Galactic Ganja Guide

Heavenly Hemp
Zodiac Leaves
Doctor Who Astrology
Cannastrology
Stellar Satvias and Cosmic Indicas
Celestial Cannabis: A Zodiac Journey
AstroHerbology: The Sky and The Soil: Volume 1
AstroHerbology:Celestial Cannabis:Volume 2
Cosmic Cannabis Cultivation
The Starry Guide to Herbal Harmony: Volume 1
The Starry Guide to Herbal Harmony: Cannabis Universe: Volume 2
Yugioh Astrology: Astrological Guide to Deck, Duels and more
Nightmare Mansion: Echoes of The Abyss
Nightmare Mansion 2: Legacy of Shadows
Nightmare Mansion 3: Shadows of the Forgotten
Nightmare Mansion 4: Echoes of the Damned
The Life and Banishment of Apophis: Book 2
Nightmare Mansion: Halls of Despair
Healing with Herb: Cannabis and Hydrocephalus
Planetary Pot: Aligning with Astrological Herbs: Volume 1
Fast Track to Freedom: 30 Days to Financial Independence Using AI, Assets, and Agile Hustles
Cosmic Hemp Pathways
How to Become Financially Free in 30 Days: 10,000 Paths to Prosperity
Zodiacal Herbage: Astrological Insights: Volume 1
Nightmare Mansion: Whispers in the Walls
The Daleks Invade Atlantis
Henry the hemp and Hydrocephalus

10X The Kidney Friendly Diet
Cannabis Universe: Adult coloring book

Hemp Astrology: The Healing Power of the Stars

Zodiacal Herbage: Astrological Insights: Cannabis Universe: Volume 2

Planetary Pot: Aligning with Astrological Herbs: Cannabis Universes: Volume 2

Doctor Who Meets the Replicators and SG-1: The Ultimate Battle for Survival

Nightmare Mansion: Curse of the Blood Moon

The Celestial Stoner: A Guide to the Zodiac

Cosmic Pleasures: Sex Toy Astrology for Every Sign

Hydrocephalus Astrology: Navigating the Stars and Healing Waters

Lapis and the Mischievous Chocolate Bar

Celestial Positions: Sexual Astrology for Every Sign

Apophis's Shadow Work Journal: **:** A Journey of Self-Discovery and Healing

Kinky Cosmos: Sexual Kink Astrology for Every Sign

Digital Cosmos: The Astrological Digimon Compendium

Stellar Seeds: The Cosmic Guide to Growing with Astrology

Apophis's Daily Gratitude Journal

Cat Astrology: Feline Mysteries of the Cosmos

The Cosmic Kama Sutra: An Astrological Guide to Sexual Positions

Unleash Your Potential: A Guided Journal Powered by AI Insights

Whispers of the Enchanted Grove

Cosmic Pleasures: An Astrological Guide to Sexual Kinks

369, 12 Manifestation Journal

Whisper of the nocturne journal(blank journal for writing or drawing)

The Boogey Book

Locked In Reflection: A Chastity Journey Through Locktober

Generating Wealth Quickly:How to Generate $100,000 in 24 Hours

Star Magic: Harness the Power of the Universe

The Flatulence Chronicles: A Fart Journal for Self-Discovery

The Doctor and The Death Moth

Seize the Day: A Personal Seizure Tracking Journal

The Ultimate Boogeyman Safari: A Journey into the Boogie World and Beyond

Whispers of Samhain: 1,000 Spells of Love, Luck, and Lunar Magic: Samhain Spell Book

Apophis's guides:Witch's Spellbook Crafting Guide for Halloween

Frost & Flame: The Enchanted Yule Grimoire of 1000 Winter Spells

The Ultimate Boogey Goo Guide & Spooky Activities for Halloween Fun

Harmony of the Scales: A Libra's Spellcraft for Balance and Beauty

The Enchanted Advent: 36 Days of Christmas Wonders

Nightmare Mansion: The Labyrinth of Screams

Harvest of Enchantment: 1,000 Spells of Gratitude, Love, and Fortune for Thanksgiving

The Boogey Chronicles: A Journal of Nightly Encounters and Shadowy Secrets

The 12 Days of Financial Freedom: A Step-by-Step Christmas Countdown to Transform Your Finances

Sigil of the Eternal Spiral Blank Journal

A Christmas Feast: Timeless Recipes for Every Meal

Holiday Stress-Free Solutions: A Survival Guide to Thriving During the Festive Season

Yu-Gi-Oh! Holiday Gifting Mastery: The Ultimate Guide for Fans and Newcomers Alike

Holiday Harmony: A Hydrocephalus Survival Guide for the Festive Season

Celestial Craft: The Witch's Almanac for 2025 – A Cosmic Guide to Manifestations, Moons, and Mystical Events

Doctor Who: The Toymaker's Winter Wonderland

Tulsa King Unveiled: A Thrilling Guide to Stallone's Mafia Masterpiece

Pendulum Craft: A Complete Guide to Crafting and Using Personalized Divination Tools

Nightmare Mansion: Santa's Eternal Eve

Starlight Noel: A Cosmic Journey through Christmas Mysteries

The Dark Architect: Unlocking the Blueprint of Existence

Surviving the Embrace: The Ultimate Guide to Encounters with The Hugging Molly

The Enchanted Codex: Secrets of the Craft for Witches, Wiccans, and Pagans

Harvest of Gratitude: A Complete Thanksgiving Guide

Yuletide Essentials: A Complete Guide to an Authentic and Magical Christmas

Celestial Smokes: A Cosmic Guide to Cigars and Astrology

Living in Balance: A Comprehensive Survival Guide to Thriving with Diabetes Insipidus

Cosmic Symbiosis: The Venom Zodiac Chronicles

The Cursed Paw of Ambition

Cosmic Symbiosis: The Astrological Venom Journal

Celestial Wonders Unfold: A Stargazer's Guide to the Cosmos (2024-2029)

The Ultimate Black Friday Prepper's Guide: Mastering Shopping Strategies and Savings

Cosmic Sales: The Astrological Guide to Black Friday Shopping

Legends of the Corn Mother and Other Harvest Myths

Whispers of the Harvest: The Corn Mother's Journal

The Evergreen Spellbook

The Doctor Meets the Boogeyman

The White Witch of Rose Hall's SpellBook

The Gingerbread Golem's Shadow: A Study in Sweet Darkness

The Gingerbread Golem Codex: An Academic Exploration of Sweet Myths

The Gingerbread Golem Grimoire: Sweet Magicks and Spells for the Festive Witch

The Curse of the Gingerbread Golem

10-minute Christmas Crafts for kids

Christmas Crisis Solutions: The Ultimate Last-Minute Survival Guide

Gingerbread Golem Recipes: Holiday Treats with a Magical Twist

The Infinite Key: Unlocking Mystical Secrets of the Ages

Enchanted Yule: A Wiccan and Pagan Guide to a Magical and Memorable Season

Dinosaurs of Power: Unlocking Ancient Magick

Astro-Dinos: The Cosmic Guide to Prehistoric Wisdom

Gallifrey's Yule Logs: A Festive Doctor Who Cookbook

The Dino Grimoire: Secrets of Prehistoric Magick

The Gift They Never Knew They Needed

The Gingerbread Golem's Culinary Alchemy: Enchanting Recipes for a Sweetly Dark Feast

A Time Lord Christmas: Holiday Adventures with the Doctor

Krampusproofing Your Home: Defensive Strategies for Yule

Silent Frights: A Collection of Christmas Creepypastas to Chill Your Bones

Santa Raptor's Jolly Carnage: A Dino-Claus Christmas Tale

Prehistoric Palettes: A Dino Wicca Coloring Journey

The Christmas Wishkeeper Chronicles

The Starlight Sleigh: A Holiday Journey

Elf Secrets: The True Magic of the North Pole

Candy Cane Conjurations

Cooking with Kids: Recipes Under 20 Minutes

Doctor Who: The TARDIS Confiscation

The Anxiety First Aid Kit: Quick Tools to Calm Your Mind

Frosty Whispers: A Winter's Tale

The Infinite Key: Unlocking the Secrets to Prosperity, Resilience, and Purpose

The Grasping Void: Why You'll Regret This Purchase

Astrology for Busy Bees: Star Signs Simplified

The Instant Focus Formula: Cut Through the Noise

The Secret Language of Colors: Unlocking the Emotional Codes

Sacred Fossil Chronicles: Blank Journal

The Christmas Cottage Miracle

Feeding Frenzy: Graboid-Inspired Recipes

Manifest in Minutes: The Quick Law of Attraction Guide

The Symbiote Chronicles: Doctor Who's Venomous Journey

Think Tiny, Grow Big: The Minimalist Mindset

The Energy Key: Unlocking Limitless Motivation

New Year, New Magic: Manifesting Your Best Year Yet

Unstoppable You: Mastering Confidence in Minutes

Infinite Energy: The Secret to Never Feeling Drained

Lightning Focus: Mastering the Art of Productivity in a Distracted World

Saturnalia Manifestation Magick: A Guide to Unlocking Abundance During the Solstice

Graboids and Garland: The Ultimate Tremors-Themed Christmas Guide

12 Nights of Holiday Magic

The Power of Pause: 60-Second Mindfulness Practices

The Quick Reset: How to Reclaim Your Life After Burnout

The Shadow Eater: A Tale of Despair and Survival

The Micro-Mastery Method: Transform Your Skills in Just Minutes a Day

Reclaiming Time: How to Live More by Doing Less

Chronovore: The Eternal Nexus

The Mind Reset: Unlocking Your Inner Peace in a Chaotic World
Confidence Code: Building Unshakable Self-Belief
Baby the Vampire Terrier
Baby the Vampire Terrier's Christmas Adventure
Celestial Streams: The Content Creator's Astrology Manual
The Wealth Whisperer: Unlocking Abundance with Everyday Actions
The Energy Equation: Maximize Your Output Without Burning Out
The Happiness Algorithm: Science-Backed Steps to Joyful Living
Stress-Free Success: Achieving Goals Without Anxiety
Mindful Wealth: The New Blueprint for Financial Freedom
The Festive Flavors of New Year: A Culinary Celebration
The Master's Gambit: Keys of Eternal Power
Shadowed Secrets: Groundhog Day Mysteries
Beneath the Burrow: Lessons from the Groundhog
Spring's Whispers: The Groundhog's Prediction
The Limitless Mindset: Unlock Your Untapped Potential
The Focus Funnel: How to Cut Through Chaos and Get Results
Bold Moves: Building Courage to Live on Your Terms
The Daily Shift: Simple Practices for Lasting Transformation
The Quarter-Life Reset: Thriving in Your 20s and 30s
The Art of Shadowplay: Building Your Own Personal Myth
The Eternal Loop: Finding Purpose in Repetition
Burrowing Wisdom: Life Lessons from the Groundhog
Shadow Work: A Groundhog Day Perspective
Love in Bloom: 5-Minute Romantic Gestures
The Shadowspell Codex: Secrets of Forbidden Magick
The Burnout Cure: Finding Balance in a Busy World
The Groundhog Prophecy: Unlocking Seasonal Secrets
Nog Tales: The Spirited History of Eggnog
Six More Weeks: Embracing Seasonal Transitions
The Lumivian Chronicles: Fragments of the Fifth Dimension

Money on Your Mind: A Beginner's Guide to Wealth
The Focus Fix: Breaking Through Distraction
January's Spirit Keepers: Mystical Protectors of the Cold
Creativity Unchained: Unlocking Your Wildest Ideas in 2025
Manifestation Mastery: 365 Days to Rewrite Your Reality
The Groundhog's Mirror: Reflecting on Change
The Weeping Angels' Christmas Curse
Burrowed in Time: A Groundhog Day Journey
Heartbeats: Poems to Share with Your Valentine
Dino Wicca: The Sacred Grimoire of Prehistoric Magick
Courage of the Pride: Finding Your Inner Roar
The Lion's Leap: Bold Moves for Big Results
Healthy Hustle: Achieving Without Overworking
Practical Manifesting: Turning Dreams into Reality in 2025
Jurassic Pharaohs: Unlocking the Magick of Ancient Egypt and Dino Wicca
The Happiness Equation: Small Changes for Big Joy
The Confidence Compass: Finding Your Inner Strength
Whispers in the Hollow: Tales of the Forgotten Beasts
Echoes from the Hollow: The Return of Forgotten Beasts
The Hollow Ascendant: The Rise of the Forgotten Beasts
The Relationship Reset: Building Better Connections
Mastering the Morning: How to Win the Day Before 8 AM
The Shadow's Dance: Groundhog Day Symbolism
Cupid's Kitchen: Quick Valentine's Day Recipes
Valentine's Day on a Budget: Love Without Breaking the Bank
Astrocraft: Aligning the Stars in the World of Minecraft
Forecasting Life: Groundhog Day Reflections

Bleeding Hearts: Twisted Tales of Valentine's Terror

Herbal Smoke Revolution: The Ultimate Guide to Nature's Cigarette Alternative

Winter's Wrath: The Complete Survival Blueprint for Extreme Freezes.

The Groundhog's Shadow: A Tale of Seasons
Burrowed Insights: Wisdom from the Groundhog
Sensual Strings: The Art of Erotic Bondage
Whispered Flames: Unlocking the Power of Fire Play
Forgotten Shadows: A Guide to Cryptids Lost to Time
Six Weeks of Secrets: Groundhog Day's Hidden Messages
Shadows and Cycles: Groundhog Day Reflections
The Art of Love Letters: Crafting the Perfect Message
Romantic Getaways at Home: Turning Your Space into Paradise
Purrfect Brews: A Cat Lover's Guide to Coffee and Companionship
The Groundhog's Wisdom: Timeless Lessons for Modern Life
The Shadow Oracle: Groundhog Day as a Predictor
Emerging from the Burrow: A Journey of Renewal
The Language of Love: Learning Your Partner's Love Style
Authorpreneur: The Ultimate Blueprint for Writing, Publishing, and Thriving as an Author
Weathering the Seasons: Groundhog Day Perspectives
Valentine's Day Magic: A Guide to Romantic Rituals
The Shadow Chronicles: Stories of Groundhog Day
Love and Laughter: Fun Games for Valentine's Day
AstroRealty: Unlocking the Stars for Property Success
The Groundhog's Path: A Guide to Seasonal Balance
Groundhog Day Diaries: Reflections in the Shadow
The Groundhog's Light: Illuminating the Path Ahead
Valentine's Traditions from Around the World
AI Wealth Revolution: Unlocking the Trillionaire Mindset
Love Rekindled: Reigniting Passion in Relationships
Single and Thriving: Self-Love on Valentine's Day
Emerald Legends: Mystical Tales of Ireland
Green Alchemy: Harnessing Nature's Magic
The Hearts of Horror: A Valentine's Day Nightmare

The Leprechaun's Guide to Wealth and Wisdom
Dancing with the Sidhe: Celebrating the Otherworld
Shamrocks and Shadows: Mysteries of the Green Isle
Emerald Energy: Harnessing Luck and Growth
The Gingerbread Golem's Valentine: A Sweetheart's Guide to Love and Enchantment
The Celtic Knot: Weaving Life and Destiny
Green Fire: Elemental Magic for St. Patrick's Day
Clover Chronicles: Finding Your Inner Luck
Ireland's Mystical Creatures: A Field Guide
Gingerbread Golem's Love Almanac
Prowl and Thrive: The Lion's Guide to Success
Love Alchemy: Transforming Your Life Through Heart Energy
WORLD DOMINATION: Woman's Rule 3:The New Life
The Midnight Rose: A Guide to Lunar Love Spells
The Forbidden Letters: Writing Your Own Love Prophecy
Luck and Lore: St. Patrick's Day for Modern Mystics
The Green Path: A Pagan Celebration of Renewal
The Dark Architect's Guide to Reprogramming Reality
Prankster's Paradise: A Guide to Harmless Hijinks
Manifest Your Reality: The Law of Attraction Simplified
The TARDIS Owner's Manual: Understanding the Doctor's Ship: *A complete guide to the TARDIS, its technology, secrets, and mysteries*
Starlit Romance: Astrology Secrets for Finding True Love
The Time Lord's Atlas: A Complete Guide to the Whoniverse: ***A breakdown of the locations, planets, and dimensions explored in Doctor Who***
Sweetheart Shadows: The Dark Side of Love and Attraction
February Fire: Reigniting Passion in Every Area of Life
The Self-Love Toolkit: 5 Ways to Embrace Who You Are
February Sparks: Ignite Your Dreams in 28 Days

March to Success: A 31-Day Action Blueprint
Ancient Paths: The 13 Sacred Principles of Dino Wicca
Echoes of Tomorrow: Navigating the AI Revolution
The Wellness Blueprint: Balancing Mind, Body, and Soul
Green Horizons: Sustainable Living for a Better Tomorrow
The AI Wealth Code: How to Make Millions with Automation
AI-Powered Creativity: Writing, Art, and Music for Profit
Extinction Rites: Rebirthing Your Soul Through Prehistoric Magick
Sacred Serpents tarot
Celestial Enchantment blank journal
Star Strains
Culinary Journeys: Exploring Global Flavors at Home
The Hollowvale Curse
The Hollowvale Harvest
The Egg of Transformation: Awakening Your Inner Power
Blooming Into Power: A Wiccan Guide to Spring Awakening
The Nightmare Nexus: The Third Doctor's Perilous Haunting
Digital Detox: Reclaiming Your Life in a Connected World
Ostara's Path: Walking the Spiral of Renewal
The Sacred Hare
Financial Freedom: Building Wealth in the Modern Age
Spring's Cauldron: Stirring the Waters of Change
The Hollowvale Pact
Quantum Consciousness: The Science of Reality Shifting
The Hollowvale Hunger
The Sacred Waters Within: A Witch's Guide to Hydrocephalus Magick
The Raven's Nest: Building a Life of Unshakable Stability
AI and the Human Mind: The Future of Intelligence
The Hollowvale Reckoning
Timeless Love: Building and Maintaining Lasting Relationships

The Raven's Roar: Unlocking Unstoppable Confidence

Raven Sight: Awakening Intuition and Inner Wisdom

The Butterfly Effect: Small Changes, Big Transformations

Taming the Boogeyman: How to Conquer Your Inner Fears

The Magick of Green: Awakening Earth's Energy in You

The Entrepreneurial Mindset: Secrets to Business Success

The Hollowvale End

The Shadow Luck Ritual: Reclaiming Power from Your Dark Side

Spring Magick for Beginners: A Simple Guide to Seasonal Energy Work

Doctor Who: The Hollowvale Conundrum

The March of Miracles: Unlocking Synchronicities in Spring

Unveiling the Cosmos: A Guide to Stargazing and Space Exploration

The Ultimate Guide to Surviving an Economic Collapse

The AI Gold Rush: How to Profit from the AI Revolution

Bastet's Shadow: The Hidden Power of Feline Magick

The Bastet Codex: Unlocking the Goddess's Magickal Secrets

Purring Spells: Harnessing Bastet's Healing Frequencies

Bastet's Nine Lives: Rebirth, Transformation, and Immortality Spells

Primal Currents: Hydrocephalus Magick in the Path of Dino Wicca

The Digital Gold Rush: Mastering E-Commerce and Online Sales

Future Shock: Adapting to the Next Decade of Change

The Quantum Mindset: Think Like a Billionaire

Sacred Motherhood: Awakening the Divine Feminine Within

The Mother's Spellbook: Enchantments for Love, Protection, and Prosperity

The Witch's Guide to Parenting: Raising Empowered and Intuitive Children

The Magick of Motherhood: Reclaiming Your Power Through Rituals

The Pagan Path to Self-Love: A Goddess's Guide to Worth and Confidence

Wild Woman Magick: Unleashing Your Primal Power

If you want solar for your home go here: https://www.harborsolar.live/apophisenterprises/

Get Some Tarot cards: https://www.makeplayingcards.com/sell/apophis-occult-shop

Get some shirts: https://www.bonfire.com/store/apophis-shirt-emporium/

<u>Instagrams:</u>
@apophis_enterprises,
@apophisbookemporium,
@apophisscardshop
Twitter: @apophisenterpr1
Tiktok:@apophisenterprise
Youtube: @sg1fan23477, @FiresideRetreatKingdom
Hive: @sg1fan23477
CheeLee: @SG1fan23477

Podcast: Apophis Chat Zone: https://open.spotify.com/show/5zXbrCLEV2xzCp8ybrfHsk?si=fb4d4fdbdce44dec

Newsletter: https://apophiss-newsletter-27c897.beehiiv.com/

If you want to support me or see posts of other projects that I have come over to: **buymeacoffee.com/mpetchinskg**

I post there daily several times a day

Get your Dinowicca or Christmas themed digital products, especially Santa Raptor songs and other musics. Here: **https://sg1fan23477.gumroad.com**

Apophis Yuletide Digital has not only digital Christmas items, but it will have all things with Dinowicca as well as other Digital products.

www.ingramcontent.com/pod-product-compliance
Lightning Source LLC
LaVergne TN
LVHW022006200926
848481LV00007B/2261